Discover Series
MARIPOSA

Spanish Edition

Archiearis Parthenias

Archon Apollinus

Battus polydamas

Morpho azul

Callosamia angulifera

Catocala sponsa

Arco de chryso

Colias erate

Danaus plexippus

Limenitis arthemis Astyanax

Liminitis bredowii

Liminitis lorquini

Nymphalis milberti

Papilio glaucus

Papilio machaon

Papilio polyxenes

Parnissius phoebus

Phragmatobia luctifera

Pieris brassicae

Pyrrhia umbra

Vanessa cardui

Watsonarctia casta

Zerynthia polyxena

Make Sure to Check Out the Other Discover Series Books from Xist Publishing:

Published in the United States by Xist Publishing
www.xistpublishing.com
PO Box 61593 Irvine, CA 92602

© 2017 First Spanish Edition by Xist Publishing
Spanish Translation by Victor Santana
All rights reserved
No portion of this book may be reproduced without express permission of the publisher
All images licensed from Fotolia

ISBN: 978-1-53240-236-4 EISBN: 978-1-53240-177-0

Xist Publishing